I0158310

# The Essential Pointers
# From
# The Lazy Man's Way
# To Enlightenment

David A. Bhodan

Right Now
Publishing

Right Now Publishing
ISBN-13:978-0692713419
ISBN-10:0692713417

Copyright © 2015 David A. Bhodan

All Rights Reserved. No part of this publication may be reproduced in any form or by any means, including scanning, photocopying, recording, taping, or by an information storage retrieval system (or otherwise) without prior written permission of the copyright holder.

First Printing, May 2016
Printed in the United States of America

All suffering is personal.

When it is clearly seen that there is no person present, how can suffering arise?

# Table of Contents

# Note To The Reader

This is for the ripe reader who is seeking 'cliff notes' for "The Lazy Man's Way To Enlightenment."

A word of caution: reading the pages that follow will have a mind-stopping effect, yet YOU eternally remain as the One effortlessly witnessing the mind go quiet.

Enjoy it. Rest in that.

Kindly consider this small offering as a benevolent bludgeoning of Truth, if you will.

Do not worry; you won't end up a bloody mess.

But you might end up in full recognition of what you've always been.

Who can say?

**David A. Bhodan**
**August 19, 2015**

## chapter 1
# Look For Yourself

You are invited to investigate and see if there actually is a seeker looking for Enlightenment. You'll be encouraged to drop all conceptual knowledge for the purpose of discovering the non-conceptual Reality You Are. When you discard all belief and opinion – and what others have told you – *and find out in your own direct experience,* you may get a taste of the essence of Reality beyond words.

You won't 'get' anything here for there is nothing to get. Clearly, this is about losing something. There isn't anything of real significance here for the mind to chew on, so you can let the mind do its thing. In fact, you won't find much food here for the mind.

Please don't expect this to be logical and reasonable; this is anything *but* logical and reasonable. The good news is, there is absolutely nothing wrong with you, and there is absolutely nothing that needs to be worked through or changed in order to see what you've always been. Leave the mind be. There is nowhere to go, and nothing to accomplish. All you need 'do' is simply recognize You already Are that which you seek.

Falling into the silent and empty ground of being, prior to experience – and under-lying all experience – you may get a taste of what's Immediate and Primary. Are You not always present, before, during and after every thought, feeling, sound, sensation and experience, no matter how 'good' or 'bad?'

See what is present before, during and after each sensation, thought and experience. See what already deeply accepts everything as it is, before the mind starts to label and resist. See what never leaves, while all else comes and goes.

You are the Wordless Reality that never comes and goes, the Empty Space where all words appear and disappear. See that You don't ever come and go. See that You were present from the beginning – even before the beginning – and wake up to the dream, the lazy man's way.

The reality is, enlightenment is beyond any

notion of a 'you' that can achieve anything. It's beyond any notion of becoming or attaining a higher or better version of you. Enlightenment is right here, right now – and it *is* what you already are, regardless of whether it's been realized or not.

This is about waking up *to* the dream. Your Real Identity is prior to the body/mind. Your Real Identity is that which the dream appears in. Thinking that the ego-personality can become enlightened is a cunning and deceptive way for the ego to postpone its own unmasking.

Make no mistake about it: To awaken to what you are – and for Liberation to occur, a shift in perception must happen. And it's never merely conceptual, but it's *always* experiential. Paradoxically, it is not an experience, for all experiences have a beginning, middle and end. It is not a particular experience among other experiences, but the ground of all experience.

You are not the story of your race, your income level, or religion affiliation. You are not your past or future successes or failures, sexual orientation and intellectual capacity. You are not your happy or sad childhood. In fact, you are none of these "things." You are no-thing.

All the authentic spiritual teachers, sages and mystics have been reminding us that in reality, you are not the separate person you appear to be, but the immense ocean of consciousness in which every manifest wave of thought, sensation and experience, appears and disappears in. You are the time-less and space-less capacity for all of life to unfold, including the appearance of a separate person.

Underneath the roles we play as mothers, fathers, wives, husbands, brothers, sisters, friends, teachers, students, business owners, employees, etc., is our True Identity. Like waves in the ocean of life, we may have different shapes and sizes. We may have different roles, beliefs, conditioning, opinions, skills and abilities. And while we may be unique expressions in the ocean of consciousness, our Real Essence is Singular and exactly the same.

Identified with the mind, I naturally avoid pain and seek pleasure. Invariably, my energy and attention is focused on defending the current image I have of myself. It doesn't always work, but that's what I am inclined to do. Little do I realize that an image isn't real; little do I see that I'm looking in the wrong direction.

In reality, it is simply the One Being playing the game of being "other," in order to recognize and remember that there is no other.  It is the One Being allowing itself to forget itself, in order to play the game of pretending to be an individual.

So, let me ask you. Who do you think you are? Who are you REALLY? Are you that person staring back in the mirror? Is what you see in the mirror the same thing as what is peering through those eyes at the mirror? What I am looking out of is different from what I am looking at in the mirror.

Whatever you can know about your 'self' is an object and therefore, isn't it. Whatever you can see, think and feel about your 'self' are also objects and therefore, isn't it, either.  What can be seen, felt or known isn't it.  Ego is a perceived object, and not the perceiving awareness. What is doing the seeing is Aware Spirit, which all objects seen appear in.

Mistakenly identified with what can be seen, felt and known, we have confused what we are with objects in perception, instead of that which is doing the perceiving. An ego personality is an object and isn't what you really are. If it can be noticed, it can't be what you are.

Does it make sense to find out who you believe you are right now, in order to discover, beyond belief, what you really are? Don't most of us believe we were created on a particular date in time, born of two parents, given a name, live for a particular time period, experience the full gamut of highs and lows, and then perish like so many before?

Most of us live out our entire lives not knowing Who We Really Are, dismissing the significance of it to the background of our awareness. Only when we deeply inquire into our beliefs and assumptions about who we think we are, do we remotely give ourselves the chance to see *what* we really are.

If we allow our beliefs about ourselves to go unquestioned, and if we naively follow what others tell us, we can be sure most of us have unnecessary drama and a good amount of inner division in our future – a future, by the way, that doesn't exist other than in our minds.

The moment we follow anyone else, in that moment, Truth begins to elude us.

If we take ourselves to be a separate individual living for certain number of years, only to end up taking the proverbial dirt nap, we're forever mistaking ourselves to *be* our body/mind. With this identification comes a natural inclination to avoid pain and gain pleasure, a surefire recipe for *more* pain and less pleasure.

Have you ridden enough on the wheel of suffering, or do you want more?

When we forget our essential insep-arability from Life itself, and identify as the limited time-bound image of 'me,' we feel homesick, seemingly far from the One we are. And then the search begins. We seek that One in time – looking for respect, fortune, love, enlightenment, or whatever we think will deliver us home. All the while, we're already Home.

Everything experienced is referred to this reference point you call "you," is it not? Understand that all problems arise from a belief in the idea of a separate "me" that must bring about a sense of alienation and confusion. This unquestioned belief in separation is the cause of all your problems.

Hence, the underlying cause is the belief in a "me" independent of other "me's" – and the affects are "my" unhappiness, "my" anxiety, "my" fear and "my" anger. As a result, we set out to become happier, more balanced, more courageous and more peaceful, further cementing the endless illusory cycle we're trapped in.

To be free of suffering, all we need do is look and see if there is anyone here separate from anything at all, including the world that is perceived with our limited senses. Looking beyond appearances, what do we find? If we don't look, we firmly believe, without investigation, that we *are* the ego personality, separate from other personalities living *in* this world.

What if the wholeness and peace we seek is already fully present, contained in every aspect of experience – and all that appears in our experience? What if who you really are was never an individual person living in this world, but the open space of welcoming awareness in which the *appearance of an individual* appears in?

When we mistake words for the actual, we unwittingly lie to ourselves. We deceive ourselves without ever realizing it – and we do it often. In a trance-like state, rarely do we question whether the words we use are anything but a fiction. Fictions are illusory – and illusion hurts. Have you noticed? It's plain and simple; words only point.

The heart of the matter here is simply (and effortlessly) seeing what's already so – and recognizing what you really are, non-conceptually.  You are prior to, and beyond the formation of words and concepts. Before words, You Are.

Can you admit to yourself that perhaps you really don't know who you are?  Can you admit to yourself that maybe all your beliefs, assumptions and opinions you have about yourself and God might simply just be that – beliefs, assumptions and opinions?

Can you acknowledge the fear and discomfort at the thought of letting all your beliefs, assumptions and opinions go? Can you acknowledge the potential difficulty in letting go of your entire investment in your God? If you can, can you then meet that fear and discomfort without trying to alter it?

So much of our esteem and identity is wrapped up in where we've been, where we are, what we've achieved, and where we plan to be some day. When a future self is imagined, it's always a present experience. When a past self is remembered, it's always a present experience. It's always right now.

Past and future "selves" are merely concepts in the mind, without any reality at all – and yet these imaginings have a tendency to torture us until we see them for what they really are – arbitrary and imagined criteria to meet in order to feel good about who we are.

If sensations are already happening, resisting what's already happening isn't the most rational and sane thing to do, is it? Can any present happening be any different than it is? Despite what the mind says, no, it cannot.

Few are ready to hear that there isn't an afterlife, because there isn't a "before" life. Afterlife implies time when there isn't any. Life, what you are, is eternal and always outside the stream of time. Instead of worrying about an afterlife, wouldn't it make sense to find out what you are right now?

Most ego-personalities cling to the concept of an afterlife in an attempt to ensure its survival after the body dies. It wants the comfort and security thinking it's going somewhere after physical death. Funny thing is, ego (the mind) does die with the body! So the thing you desire to continue on after the body dies (mind) is toast! In fact, it never existed in the first place. What a waste of energy, don't you think?

As Jesus said, *"Unless you become like a little child, you will never enter the Kingdom of Heaven."* You must enter completely naked.

The price of admission is all about a loss – a profound loss that, believe it or not, you won't miss or regret losing.

It's a stripping away of all the false ideas – especially the existence of time and being an individual. Like a ball of twine unraveled, nothing is left but a timeless, awake, aware, empty space of knowing, where everything appears and disappears in.

That's what you are; Timeless, Changeless Empty Being – yet full of the changing, passing scene. Being open to the real possibility that there is no "you" living a life, but that Life is living itself through you, as you, is the ticket that buys you entry.

So, are you ready to lose your entire world? Losing our entire world for the sake of gaining the whole world is requisite. As Jesus said, *"Die before you die."* What he was pointing to was the death of the "you" you think you are.

The discovery of truth is clearly in the discernment of the false. Peel away all that is untrue and what remains is true. Like an onion, what is left when you peel away all the layers? Just pure empty space, that's all. But different than a peeled onion, this space is empty, knowing and aware.

Realization does not come from personal effort, belief or any quality of thinking.

When we allow what is to be as it is, we give ourselves the opportunity to transcend dualism, at the same including dualism. Seeing beyond belief and dualism, our limited senses are transcended – and it is seen that all arises in the non-dual Awareness that everything is dependent on.

Nothing can stand independent of the awareness that perceives it.  When this isn't truly seen, you completely miss out on the discovery of what you really are.

Let go of all expectations and demands. Expectations and demand presumes – and Reality doesn't. Come innocent and pure. Give up your habitual attachment to struggle and effort for the sake of directly experiencing the peace beyond understanding, the joy without cause you are.

## chapter 2
# Behind The Mind

You are prior to all mental constructions, at the same time allowing all mental constructions. You are the un-construct that allows all construction. You have no real life story; your apparent individual story is allowed in what you really are.

Self-knowledge is simply investigating, like a scientist, into the ideas and notions about what you believe yourself to be, and allowing for the possibility that none of it is true, now or ever.

Emptied of all notions, consider that all along, you've been whole and complete, never lacking a thing. Consider the possibility who you really are has never been a limited, finite being with a certain life span, here to live for a while only to die.

Consider the possibility that Life is complete as it is, and that within each moment, Reality is infinitely manifesting. All the apparent parts are nothing other than an expression of one magnificent Whole – and You Are That.

In the end, what is realized is that Liberation is a total poverty, a total loss of *everything*. Liberation is a total loss of individuality and separation – and belief in anything the mind comes up with, so that nothing but what you are remains.

This is what Christ was referring to when he said it is more difficult for a rich man to enter the kingdom of heaven than for a camel to pass through the eye of a needle.

When all is lost, and when you empty yourself, there is just fullness. When there is nothing left, there is just Completeness, Wholeness.

Awareness is all there is.  You are Awareness Itself, not somebody who is aware.

Enlightenment is rather simple. It's really nothing more than remembering some-thing forgotten. It is nothing more, or other than, the realization of the true nature of Reality.

Liberation is the spontaneous cognition and remembrance that separation and individuality are both illusory. Enlightenment knows the mind is an object in awareness, an appearance on the screen of the Changeless Reality You Are.

Enlightenment is the absence of any separate individual entity we call a person. Therefore, no one becomes enlightened. If anyone proclaims to be enlightened, simply nod your head and walk the other way.

And it has nothing to do with you or me. It's not a state of mind, and it is not an experience! It has absolutely nothing to do with mystical experiences or bliss. It's not about a special state of being, but it has everything to do with the natural state of being.

There isn't anything for the ego in enlightenment. This is why most aren't ready for this radical message, precisely *because* there is nothing for sale. There's nothing to 'get' or 'possess.' Most are only ready for a message that makes sense to the mind – and this message, this sharing, makes absolutely no sense at all to the mind!

After reading this book, most will go back to looking for something they can 'know' and 'do' – something that involves effort towards becoming something more, better or different. Some will file this away as hogwash, claiming that it just can't be this simple.

Minds love – and are drawn to, ideas of extraordinary powers, abilities and ways of being. Minds aren't particularly interested in "what is, as it is" because there's nothing really special about what is. Clouds tend to draw more attention than the empty sky. Minds want the noisy, glowing fireworks!

The mind only understands the rational, logical and linear – and this is anything but that. Minds are interested in (and can only understand) progressive paths, processes and journeys towards becoming some-thing other, or more, than it already is.

The mind can only comprehend that which is in time. Enlightenment, or the realization-discovery of who you really are is outside of time, prior to time.

Reality is undivided and boundless, and *is* what you are. Sharing this with others need never be exaggerated, embellished or adorned, for that would be too much. It is so ordinary – and without the bells and whistles – that it is literally beyond comprehension. It is so much less than the mind could ever imagine; it can never *be* what the mind imagines.

Despite what many may imagine, it doesn't point to a permanent state of happiness, or an eternal sense of being beyond human pain and drama. The primary difference is that there is no longer identification with being a particular body-mind, apart from other body-minds. Without a reference point, things like pain and discomfort don't hang around long.

I used to think that peace and surrender was something I had to "do" – and that they were states I could reach. However, what was discovered was that peace and surrender was already present before I went in search of it. They were both present realities that went overlooked. The knowing or 'seeing' of this *is* the peace that surpasses all understanding.

The amazing paradox is that there is nobody here separate from this moment that *can* surrender to this moment, and yet, a deep surrender of this moment is already occurring. All thought, sensation, sound and experience are already being allowed in the impartial Space That You Are.

Peace and love are both present moment realities, aspects of what you really are. They never need to be attained or acquired. Seeking peace and love is to deny its presence. Before we seek peace and love, we can simply notice if it's not already present. It is.

Enlightenment is the realization that Life is unfolding as it is – and cannot unfold any other way, regardless of what the mind has to say. As the Jesuit priest Anthony de Mello once said, *"Enlightenment is the absolute cooperation with the inevitable."*

You can only *be* what you are; you cannot know what you are. The Subject, what you are, can never be known, for it would have to be an object. Only an object can be known. You can only know what is not. What is – you can only be.

Whatever you think it is, that's not it; it is entirely and absolutely different from that. Enlightenment, eternally beyond thought, can never be what you think.

The truth is, belief is forever married to doubt. Belief and doubt reside on the same restless coin. If you believe something, it means you really don't know – and there is nothing wrong with that. The problem arises when we think our belief establishes truth. Problems arise when we think we know. Problems arise when we resist the unknown – which is what we are.

Beliefs are mental constructs created in the mind in order to feel in control of our world. Beliefs are spontaneously created in the mind – and then we take ownership of them, claiming they are "our" beliefs. However, they get created all on their own, without us!

We end up depending on beliefs to tell us how life really is, instead of relying on our actual and lived experience to tell us what's really so. Beliefs ultimately fail to provide us the security we seek, because they *can't ever provide* the security we seek.

You already are the Security you seek.

Faith is merely belief – and in its best form, it becomes trust. You can spin it anyway you want with clever words, supreme logic and reason, but in the end, you just don't know.

In the midst of existential discomfort and pervasive doubt, people make statements like, "You just have to believe," "It's all God's will," "It's not up to me, because God is in control." In their fear of losing control, they immediately go right back to trying to manipulate the outcome to their liking, further cementing the notion that they are separate individuals *in* control.

If everything you presently "know" and believe still hasn't revealed what you're looking for, then doesn't it follow that the unknown is where your answer lies?

Only when you stop insisting that your beliefs establish what's true, will you have the opportunity to realize what's true – about yourself and everything else.

This desire to know what you are must be greater than your fear of giving up your lifetime investment in your beliefs about who you are. This is essential.

The value of any realization, insight or understanding is only ever in this fresh and new moment. Yesterday's realization isn't fresh. Yesterday is past and we're back in memory again, raising the dead. Clinging to old insights and beliefs is like dancing with the dead. Life is only ever now.

At some point, usually when we've reached the end of our emotional rope – or perhaps when we're ripe enough, we have the opportunity to reorient our priorities away from achievements we think we need to attain in order to be happy and secure – to finding out who it is that's chasing the achievements in the first place.

Only when we pause long enough can we see we're like a dog chasing its tail, never seeing we're already in possession of what we're chasing! Only an earnest examination into the very nature of our essence will do. Spiritual liberation is all about discovering the eternal, animating essence beneath and behind changing appearances – and not stopping *at* changing appearances.

## chapter 3
# On Present Evidence

If you say you are the silent witness, what notices that silent witness? Can you find the subject that is aware of the silent witness? Can you say anything about it? Anything you can say about it must mean it is an object in awareness and isn't the Ultimate Reality.   Therefore, the silent witness is an object to You.

What you are can't be found, yet what you are is always Here.

The usefulness of sitting in silence lies in the opportunity to still thinking, and to recognize your true nature, that which is prior to thinking. It's an opportunity to see what thinking arises in. And yet, You have this opportunity in each moment, regardless of meditation, regardless of how much noise is present, and regardless of the conditions present.

If you look for the one who is supposedly "having" a present experience, the one who is assumed to be "doing" the thinking, seeing and hearing – can you actually find anyone at the center?  On present evidence, can you even pinpoint a center?

Simply look with naked awareness, and see if you can find any solid entity you can call "you" separate from anything else.

Look for the person you think you are; can you find it?   Can you find you?

Where is this entity you call the "me" located? Where is this reference point you claim is present – you know, the reference point that everything impacts and is referred back to?  Where is it centered?  If your name is 'Joe or 'Kay,' where is Joe or Kay centrally located?   Without objectifying anything, what is seen?

Whatever you say is only a concept, a belief.   Whatever you say you are isn't what you are. It can't be. Prior to belief or concept, simply look for where you are. So, where are you?

While there may very well be an idea that there is a "me" within "my body" looking out at "the world" and directing this body/mind through life, owning thoughts, making my decisions, choosing my actions, behaviors and feelings, is there any real evidence of this to be found?

This "me" living inside a body, this "me" that is a separate unit of consciousness possessed with a soul, *is* the Immaculate Misconception!

Is there any one spot in the body where you can say, "This is what I am; this is where I start?" Is there any clear distinction between you and not you? Aside from a mental image, a thought, and a story about who you *think* you are, can it be seen that there isn't any separate entity encapsulated within a body?

The fact is, you can only *believe or assume* you are a separate entity existing *in* this world. You can't know it. Conversely, you *can* know you aren't a separate entity – and that the world is *within* what you are, but you can only believe you are an individual living in this world. Is assumption enough for you?

Why rely on anything other than your own ability to see? Take a look and see for yourself what is true in your own experience, instead of relying on beliefs, dogma, faith and tradition. It is worth reiterating: the desire to see what's real must be greater than your fear of what may happen to your investment in your beliefs!

And it's not a looking "out there" at objects in our awareness. What we are isn't an object. What we are is the Subject. It's a 180-degree turn of attention inward, to look and see what's doing the looking. In Christianity, *repent* didn't mean to atone for your sins, but to "turn your attention inward and see everything anew" – and notice what is doing the looking.

If you've been told you are this Clear, Empty, Awake and Aware Space that is eternally untouched by anything, look and see for yourself whether this is true or not. Believing in it matters not. Until you *know* first-hand, without any doubt whatsoever, you're just juggling stale concepts that have no aliveness in them. You're just hanging out at the surface, treading water.

You are the aliveness and boundlessness you seek – and until you discover this for yourself, what good is any of this to you? Why would you ever accept the word of anyone else, no matter how highly regarded they are, no matter how beautiful and flowery the words are?

Buddha or Jesus himself could show up at your doorstep and eloquently tell you wonderful things about what you are – things you've never heard – but unless YOU know, of what value are their words? Until You know, you don't know.

What you really are is the total and complete absence of fear. Notice the fear present in the questioning of what you believe is true. It's not only natural, but it is understandable, is it not? Let it be there. What you really are is the unconditional love and compassion that welcomes all fear. Just look for yourself. No one can do this for you.

Belief in the unreal divides and fractures, and there is no escaping that experience. What is real never divides, never hurts.

What is the common denominator in all your problems? Isn't it the "you," the "me", the "I" you call yourself? If the "I" thought is seen to be unreal and the *cause* of all your troubles, what must happen to the effects?

When the "I" and the "me" thought are *seen* to be the products of imagination, what YOU REALLY ARE reveals itself as that which never left in the first place.

Allow your fiction to come to an end, because on the other side of your fiction is Reality, beautiful and true. In the midst of your fiction, Reality is. It's not really even accurate to say, "Allow your fiction to end." Who is present to even have a fiction?

Instead, see through the fiction. See there is no one here to *have* a fiction – and watch the fiction end.　　Within the fiction is Reality, waiting to be discovered.　There is nothing to 'get rid of.'　You need only SEE.

## chapter 4
# Within What You Are

Whatever drops away wasn't real to begin with. See this and be free.

The ego personality has the habit of claiming to be the primary seer, rejecting this and wanting that. However, being witnessed and known by YOU, the Subject, the ego personality is part of the passing scenery. If it's part of the passing scene, then it must be an object in Consciousness. Consequently, the personality, the imagined self, can never be the final Witness, just as a wave cannot see the ocean.

Awareness is not a thought or feeling. Thoughts and feelings arise in awareness. Awareness is always present, never coming or going. It is forever unharmed by thought and feeling – and is the Real.

Freedom is in the realization of the wisdom of no escape; it's in the recognition that there isn't anyone present to escape anything. This isn't about belief; this is nothing short of a radical shift in perception, beyond belief or anything the mind can ever conceive.

Without You, content-free Awareness, nothing is. Without You, pleasure and pain can't even be experienced. Pain and pleasure have no independent existence and therefore, is unreal. Emotions are objects seen, felt and known, and merely phenomena passing through the Eternal You.

For suffering to arise, the belief in the "me" must be present. In the absence of the "me," there isn't anyone taking ownership of any aspect of experience, including fear and desire. Without personal ownership, suffering can't arise.

In fact, there are no problems in presence. There are no problems unless you think about them, are there? Thinking must be present in order for suffering to happen. But what are you?

Timeless Being, here and now, is always problem free. Timeless being, the Real, is that which contains the mind that creates the problem. Minds create problems only to look for solutions for them. It's an endless loop, until it is seen for what it is, an object in the awareness you are.

All exists now. All there is – is now. There isn't a past, present and future. Thinking divides the One into the Many, and believes the now is the moment that exists between a past and future.

There is only ever now; everything else is but a dream imagined, literally. Imagination is not reality, but happens in reality. Nothing is to be rejected or accepted. Just see what is real. That is all.

See all that is false and find out what remains. What remains is the Real.

The "I" thought is the birth of fear – and fear brings about insecurity and vulnerability. Insecurity and vulnerability is the driving force behind becoming, and yet, there is no becoming in being.

Fear is born of separation, which isn't real, only imagined. Imagination imagines separation. It is an unreal thought imagining another unreal thought – within what you are, the REAL.

There is nothing wrong with desire. Humans desire; it comes with the package. Attachment to desire is the cause of suffering. There isn't anything wrong with desire, but see every "thing" you desire is imaginary. Every "thing" you fear is imaginary.

We seek because we feel separate – and we feel separate when we seek. We feel separate from each other and from life, but are we really separate? What speaks of this separation?  Can we find it in nature? Are boundaries actually real - or are they simply imagined products of the mind designed to divide and separate?

All there is, is Wholeness – the One, Infinite Energy appearing as everything ... the oceans, the sky, human beings, cars, horns honking, grass growing, trees blooming, leaves falling, birds chirping, bees stinging, babies crying, lovers arguing and enemies killing – and *whatever* else you can come up with.  It is the Inexpressible No-thing appearing as absolutely Every-thing.

All content arises liberated. In other words, all things appear dualistically with an opposite, and what appears is already free. Love arises in unison with fear, always. Peace arises in unison with conflict, always. In order to experience peace, one must be able to experience conflict. In order to experience love, fear must be a potential experience.

Since the mind can only think dualistically, it divides everything up into a subject - object split. Everything becomes about "me" experiencing this that I like and this that I don't like. And the quality of my experience is determined mostly by experiencing what I want through effort and achievement – and avoiding what I don't want with resistance and denial.

And yet, the "me" isn't what will experience the peace and freedom it longs for. Egos don't get to experience peace and freedom. True and total freedom has nothing to do with getting rid of our human weaknesses and perceived imperfections.    Rather, it is the full embrace of them, as they are.

With a sense of separation comes a certain degree of dissatisfaction – a sense that something is missing.  We can't ever put our finger on what is missing, but we just know something isn't right, or we wouldn't be feeling dissatisfied, longing for something different than what we have.

The only problem we ever have is when we want something different than what we already have.

Only when there is an opening to the possibility of that which is beyond self-centered thinking, can the contracted energy dissolve back into the unbounded freedom it already is. Until then, it's simply boundless energy allowing itself to be bound, all within the appearance of a particular body/mind, within the freedom You Already Are.

The idea of someone who needs to be liberated from something drops away in the simple seeing that there never was anyone who needed anything. The dream of separation ends upon the full recognition that All is One. Struggle and effort drop away quite naturally. Who is present to struggle and strive for that which never left in the first place?

Timeless Being requires no path to it. It's Here, now. Presence of Being demands nothing. It is the Gentle Constant where all demands and requirements arise in. It sits back and enjoys its own show. It is the writer, producer, actors, the stage and the screen upon which it plays. It sits back in wonder and curiosity, celebrating its own Play.

Time is mind.  The belief in time, coupled with the belief in separation and individuality can be said to be the cause of all your troubles.  To awaken to what you are is to literally awaken *from* time – and to *see* there is only ever a timeless now.

Now implies a moment between a past and a future, but now isn't sandwiched between the last moment and the next moment.  There is just what is happening.

Past is memory only and future is anticipation or imagination.  Both are mental concepts believed to be real. Granted, it appears that there is a past and future, but Reality is beyond time and appearances – and always now.

We bring a dead thing to life through our resistance, judgment, and wishing it was different than it is. This is the energy that feeds and gives life to the dead, resurrecting what already disappeared. Resurrecting the dead never feels quite right, because it's illusory. All the while, we continue to reinforce the sense of "me" that is experiencing all that.

All thought is past. As soon as it arises, it is gone. As soon as thought arises, the next sensation or thought arises, no longer to exist. All sensations are past. YOU are now. YOU *are* this moment – the timeless being in which all temporal thoughts and sensations emerge.

Without referencing thought or the past, without quoting your favorite quotes or clichés – and without memory or opinion, in this moment, right where you are, what do you know for sure? Other than the fact of being – other than the fact you are – is there anything you can know in this fresh, new moment?

If you really look deeply, it is seen you can't know anything in this moment but what you are. In this recognition, all questions and answers dissolve because Life is the answer.

To be clear, there is no "you" *and* this moment. There is no such thing as "be here now." This is a dualistic statement, for there is no "you" that *can* be here now. There is only now – and what you are *is* the timeless now, in its entirety, wholly, and without separation.

When I fear the absence of myself, I reinforce the belief in the dream of individuality, which keeps me asleep and prone to further pain and suffering. Fearing pain, I seek to gain pleasure. When I seek to gain pleasure, I am in fear of future pain. It is an endless loop in time, that is, until I recognize What I Really Am.

When I fear no longer existing, I cling to security and survival, two concepts that have no reality. Fearing my own demise, I believe in a beginning and an end. Believing in a beginning and an end, I naturally desire to postpone that end. In seeing what I am, the concepts of a beginning and an end drop away in timeless being – and You are this timeless being.

Fearing vulnerability, I strive to be strong. Fearing insecurity, I strive to be secure and project what I am not. Fearing intimacy, I strive to be indifferent. If I fear being nobody, I strive to be somebody. The things I fear seem to be in a constant shuffle, a game of musical chairs in which I am always trying to find a safe, comfortable seat.

We say, "I am afraid," but are you really the one who is afraid? Is it true that you are the one in fear? Might it be that you are simply the boundless capacity and space for fear, the vast stillness in which fear comes and goes?

If I believe I am a separate person living in this world, fear must arise. Fear is born of separation and my life becomes an ongoing negotiation and management of all that I fear. Feeling separate, I take things very personally and am inclined to compare, resist, envy and judge "others" according to my belief systems, values and opinions.

Believing that the purpose and meaning of my life is to strive to become more than I already am (and to make my life work) I am often left feeling guilty when I don't live up to the standard I set for myself. I feel guilty when I "get off track" and therefore, reinsert myself back on the path of improvement in order to become something other than what I already am.

In presence, there is no becoming. In presence, there is only now; becoming involves time. In seeing that there is no one living this life and that life is living itself through this body/mind, fear, guilt and shame drop away. When I know what I am, illusory fear, guilt and shame doesn't arise anymore. Fear, guilt and shame need time – and I am NOW, fear-less, guilt-less and time-less.

As long as I continue to pay attention and buy into my story of what 'should be' and what 'should have' happened, I remain paralyzed. As long as my energy goes into indulging in my sense of guilt and shame, I continue to sever any possibility of seeing what I am – and I remain in fear. Liberation becomes a "nice idea" for others, but not for me.  For me, liberation is just a concept.

Even fear, guilt, shame and pain want to come to rest. After expressing itself, it simply wants to rest, but we're too caught up in trying to get rid of it, numb out to it, or run away from it. Any movement is a movement away – and we lock in place what we don't want.

If our love is dependent on physical beauty, when beauty fades, our love fades. If our love is dependent on feelings, when feelings fade, our love is compromised. If our love is associated with stories, when stories are forgotten, so is our love. And if our love latches onto time and form, when form perishes, time-bound love dies, too.

Presence, prior to my story about my life, forever remains right here, right now. It is untouched by the passing show appearing in Consciousness. If the story that produced the fear and guilt is seen not to have an author, no longer is there "my" fear, "my" guilt, or "my" shame. It is simply seen for what it is, as it is – simply raw emotion emerging to express itself.

chapter 5

# One Animating Essence

The entire visible world, the world of form, is the world of the manifest. It is a world of phenomena – that which appears to be. Absolutely every "thing" is impermanent, with a beginning, middle and end – including the "you" you think you are. All appearances have a certain life span. After all, what is born must die.

You are the un-manifest, the No-thing that absolutely everything happens in. The opposite of phenomena is noumenon – which means, "that which is." That which is, the un-manifest, is the formless Reality from which every form emerges. Reality, or that which never changes, is what all phenomena comes and goes in. It is the unchanging, un-manifest Reality You Are.

The "you" that you think you are, is appearance only – happening within what you are. You are not the body, that thing in which you drive around in all day. You are not the mind, the activity of thinking that attempts to 'know' everything as it arises.

Once you really *see* appearances don't happen to "you," including thoughts, feelings and sensations, and that they happen in the empty, awake, welcoming aware space You Are, you won't care what is arising! No longer will you be identified with the body/mind that seeks pleasure and avoids pain.

Life still goes on. Life continues to happen. There can be pleasurable days and not so pleasurable days. It doesn't really matter anymore because there isn't any concern about what 'may' happen or what has already happened. Allowing what is, and resting in the unharmed awareness you are, is there a threat anymore? Who is threatened?

After all, what are they occurring to? What are they occurring in? This is all about discovering your True Identity, and not relying on a lifelong assumption of who you *think* you are.

Can the appearance of changing form impact one iota of the changeless, formless identity You Are?

The belief in the "me," that fictitious center where everything is referenced to, is the cause of all your problems. Seen through as false, watch all your problems dissolve. Once the falsity of something is seen, you can never go back to believing in it. What is seen can never be unseen. What you no longer give life to cannot survive.

Ego is simply the movement of thoughts (thinking) towards objects of perception, in the form of grasping or aversion. It is an endless loop appearing in Consciousness and fools Consciousness into a trance of identification. It is "me" that doesn't like "this" and it is "me" that must have "that," while You embrace both.

Our greatest fear is not the fear of death; it's the fear of life. It is the fear of truly living, of being alive and awake and undefined in this moment. We close off to, numb out to, and resist the "negative" experiences. But life includes absolutely everything, not just the "positive" experiences.

Unless we include the whole lot, we suffer. We can't pick and choose what we experience. To be totally alive is to recognize that we cannot protect ourselves from any of it. There is so much to be seen in the wisdom of no escape.

There is something here, right where you are, that is already free and untouched from 'me and my difficulties,' from 'me and my insecurities,' from 'me and my sadness,' and from 'me and my sense of success and failure.' There is something present before the seeming division of inside and outside, up and down, here and there.

It is present before thought; it is immediate and prior to all experience and identification. We can hear the words of the Zen Master who said, "When I heard the sound of the bell ringing, there was no I and there was no bell; there was just the ringing." In other words, there wasn't anyone separate listening to the sound of a bell. Rather, there was just immediate experience, prior to any commentary about it.

Just stay right here, right now, looking at the still, non-conceptual pause. Notice the silent, aware presence that never leaves – that everything comes and goes in. That which is always present is real. You are the Changeless Reality in which all change happens within.

Because the ultimate reality isn't anything seen, but rather that which is Seeing, it doesn't matter at all what is being seen in any moment. What is being seen is an object and you are the Subject that sees. Whether you see peace or conflict, calm or turbulence, happiness or sadness, matters not in the least; the Witnessing of these passing states is already free.

Resting in this pure and prior Witnessing, it is noticed that this Witnessing is not an experience that comes and goes, but is the vast and open expanse that allows all states to come and go in. Resting in this simple Witnessing, I am no longer pre-occupied in the search for particular experiences. I can let whatever comes come. None of it is a problem.

In truth, there is no Seer or Witness; there is simply Seeing, Witnessing – and You Are That. There is something that notices the silent seer or witness. Like light, it cannot itself be seen, but it illuminates all that is seen. We can't say it is absent, but it can never be found. This is the mystery of being conscious. We are ultimately never found, but obviously present and aware.

Whatever floats by my True Identity are like clouds floating by on a clear summer sky, and there is more than enough space in me for all of it. The most sacred and the most profane are equally welcome in the open clearing I am. The most extraordinary and ordinary are equally allowed in the space I am. What I am never moves at all. What I am is stillness itself, in which all things move. I am the unmoved mover of the world.

In my contracted state of the little me, I am 'in here' looking out at objects 'out there' – and this is the illusory divide that is the cause of all my problems. Being on this side of my face that looks out, I am in constant protection mode, attempting to experience only that which I deem comfortable and pleasurable.

Resting in what I really am, all that mental activity and resistance drops away in the thought-free expanse I am. In seeing that "inside" and "outside" are mere mental constructs – and the primary reason for the struggle, all separation dissolves back into the boundless energy I am. The sensation that once set me apart from all that was 'outside' fades into the nothingness from which it came.

Subject and object is no more. I no longer see the clouds; I am the clouds. I no longer see the sun shining; I am the sun shining. I no longer feel the breeze on my face; I am that breeze. The clouds, sun and the cool breeze are within me; they are Me. The sun isn't an object seen 'out there,' but radiates deep within my being, shining everywhere all at once.

Resting in ever-present awareness, every object is its own subject. Every arising sees itself, for *I am that arising seeing itself.* I am not looking at the moon; I am the moon that sees itself. I am not looking at the ocean; I am the ocean that sees itself. Everything still goes on just as before, but in the absence of the subject and object split that divides. And Oneness remains.

Thus, the tree is still a tree, but it's not an object being looked at, and I am not a separate subject looking at it. The tree and I simultaneously appear in the presence of awareness, already free in that expanse, arising as a non-dual movement, in a non-dual space.

Make no mistake about it, what the mind longs for and fears most at the same time is its own absence, its own disappearance as the captain steering the ship. When what *isn't* present is viewed to be more desirable than what *is* present, the actual reality of the present moment is inwardly resisted. This unquestioned belief is the fuel that drives the treadmill of suffering.

Consciousness, the All That Is, can never be oversimplified. In fact, it is simplicity itself – while the mind is complexity itself. Indivisible Consciousness can only express itself in the illusory world of polarities by pretending to be divisible. Remarkably, its fundamental nature is to be what it is by pretending to become what it is pretending to not be.

In Reality, Consciousness has no opposite and can't transform into what isn't. It is the only thing present, and always what is. Put simply, Reality is what is – and can never be what isn't. So, whenever we pretend that there is something better than what is, we never actually experience the reality of the moment as it unfolds.

You are Consciousness Itself, and you can't ever separate yourself from the Reality you already are. That would be as impossible as separating dryness from the desert, or wetness from water. You are the Light that gives life to the movie of 'your' life, always.

Waking up has nothing to do with building character, self-improvement or being the best person you can be. It has nothing to do with 'doing unto others as you would do unto you,' however, in the clear recognition of what you are, it is seen there is no "other." Consequently, when it is seen that you *are* the so-called 'other,' you realize that what you do to 'others' you in fact do to yourself.

So while you may hear that there is no right and wrong in Reality, because Reality is beyond the distinctions of right and wrong, there is, however, an ethic to enlightenment. Knowing it's all One, why would the One desire to harm Itself?

Waking up to Reality is simply about being awake and aware to what is – being present to how life actually expresses, here and now. Here and now, as it is, is the only Reality – *before* the mind labels experience as good or bad, right or wrong. While it seems mysterious, it is so unavoidably obvious. It is the open secret that everyone is looking for, but can't ever seem to find.

Allowing is not a 'doing' – it is the radically simple noticing that everything that appears in awareness is already allowed in, as it is. It could be the most joyous occasion to the most horrific tragedy. So, there is no need to 'try' and allow, but simply see that this allowing has already happened in the vastness of what you are. Nothing is denied entry. Only the mind resists what is.

Being present to what is without ever moving away from it, we recognize that it's very possible to be open to any kind of experience without crumbling inside, or feeling threatened. By simply being present to *whatever* arises, we see that when we don't resist any experience, the experience never owns us. Nothing can ever threaten what we are.

*Being with what is* brings you out of the mental realm of thinking and into the non-conceptual realm of sensory experience. No longer referencing thought to describe experience, any residual distance or separation dissolves. Consequently, experience is felt directly, without a conceptual overlay.

And so, this is never about eliminating or changing anything. It's about being awake to what is – and not thinking what isn't is it. Instead, you're in the flow of what is and yet, there isn't a 'you' in the flow of what is. That's just more duality. There is just the flow of life – and you *are* this flow, wholly and completely.

You need nothing to be happy; you need something to be sad. Unless you are fulfilled with nothing, nothing will fulfill you.

Awake to what is, there is no disillusioned or enlightened one to be found. There isn't anyone apart from That which appears as everything. There is no one present apart from the One that can always be this way or that way. In this knowing, many of the same activities can still go on, but it's evident we aren't 'doing' any of it.

Thinking happens, but is there a thinker? Don't we split it up between the thinker and the thought – as in, a thinker who thinks thoughts? Where is this thinker who thinks? Without referring to more thinking, is there a division actually present, or is it just something we've assumed for so long?

You don't 'have' thoughts; you never did. You are not the thinker of thoughts; you never were. You are the wide-open space in which all thinking arises. You are the vast empty sky that all thought-clouds form, move and dissolve in.

The reality is, we don't "think" thoughts. Thoughts arise and are witnessed by what you are, that which is prior to thinking. The Immaculate Misconception is that "we" are the ones thinking! We claim ownership of thinking and say, "I am thinking and these are my thoughts." If you believe this, you believe you *are* the mind, the thing that will one day die.

The mind is designed to divide the world and everyone in it into body, mind and soul, good and evil, right and wrong, past, present and future. All these divisions are illusory and keep the dream alive.

There is no mind per se – there is only thought arising. When there is no thinking, there is no mind. There is no hearer; there is only hearing happening, effortlessly. There is no seer; there is only effortless seeing, without a subject-object division, happening by itself. There is no lover separate from The Beloved.

When I take a look at thinking, I notice it arises spontaneously. It is so obvious and in plain view, yet it is easy to understand why most overlook it. The recognition of your total and complete freedom is closer than breathing, nearer than hands and feet. It is so close we miss it. It's so close to thinking (in fact, it's inseparable from it) that we get fused with it – and confusion ensues.

You are the thought-free capacity where thinking occurs in. As capacity, you are eternally unbounded – and already free.

The lazy man's way to enlightenment is simple, because it takes no effort at all. Effortlessly noticing what is present, prior to the commentary of the mind, is all it really takes. Oh, losing your entire world, too. Most people will never awaken to what they are simply because they cling to their illusions.

Most people won't awaken because they will continue to insist that what is happening shouldn't be happening. Most people won't awaken because they are stuck on the belief that they are the one doing the thinking, instead of noticing that thinking happens spontaneously, without 'them.' Most are deeply attached to their neurosis.

Identified as the author of thinking, people insist on trying to control or change their experience. They look to *get* something, whether it's a different experience, or a better experience. It's the 'anything but this' orientation that brings about discomfort. But awakening is completely beyond the notion of getting or changing anything.

Liberation is the seeing that "you" never thought a single thing, ever.

chapter 6

# No Boundary
# Awareness

There are not two things, a seer and a seen, in our actual experience! The seer and the seen are of one single substance and that substance is our Self, Consciousness. All objects of perception are within consciousness, are they not? Objects appear within what we are – including the body and the mind.

Looking for this Reality, looking for the animating essence in every experience of the mind, body and world, we discover Consciousness at the root, a Knowing Presence of Awareness that never leaves. In fact, we can never deny the fact of being, the fact that we know we are. Can you deny this?

Oneness created the mind to divide and separate – to only think in dualistic terms of the opposites. Everything that arises does so dualistically. Although each arising has an opposite, the actual reality is Non-dual, or One appearing as two – without an opposite. Freedom is the transcendence of the polarities, at the same time including the polarities.

This was expressed in Isaiah as *"I am the Lord, and there is nothing else."* Jesus also said in The Gospel of Saint Thomas: *"I am the Light that is above them all, I am the All,*

*the All came forth from Me and the All attained to Me. Cleave a piece of wood, I am there; Lift up the stone and you will find Me there."*

The peace and freedom longed for is about subtraction, not addition. As Jesus said, *"You must lose your life to save it." "Unless you die before you die, you will never truly live."* This is what he meant by salvation.

What Christ was pointing to is when there's no longer anyone taking ownership of life, or anyone trying to possess or avoid any experience, life is no longer something to be denied or resisted, but rather, something to be celebrated and enjoyed. Until we do, we forever remain on the wheel of suffering, running from this and chasing that.

When Christ said, *"The meek shall inherit the earth,"* he meant that only those with a deep humility will see the true nature of reality and thus, enter the kingdom of God.

This is a message from your Self to your Self: wake up from the mind. Wake up from the idea of the past and future and remember what you've always been and always will be. You are the untouched presence of awareness (Spirit) that allows absolutely everything to be.

The Absolute is the One without a second – and YOU ARE THAT ONE.

Enlightenment is the sudden realization that non-duality, not duality, is the reality of our experience. Consciousness is not private and personal, but universal and impersonal, eternally.

If indeed the Infinite Consciousness is all-encompassing, then it must be equally present in anger, fear and suffering. It's natural to want to experience Oneness in the calm of meditation, or in the beauty of the landscape, but it must also be immediately available in pain, boredom, struggle and resistance, too.

None of your 'knowledge' has brought you to the realization that You are the One that is looking through your eyes right now. Your knowledge has not brought you relief from the pain and suffering that continues to frustrate you because of your ongoing belief in who you think you are. Wisdom blooms when you finally see that all that you know hasn't delivered what you've been seeking.

The mind works in time – and in a linear fashion. It will turn anything into a dogma, and turn it into a process in time, believing the words to be the real. And those words end up torturing us, keeping us bound in time and caught between the polarities of good and bad, right and wrong, love and hate, rich and poor, worthy and unworthy, holy and unholy.

To the mind, awareness is no-thing. It is without quality, attribute, shape, form, time or age. Awareness is clear and empty, yet it is the container in which all qualities, attributes, shapes and forms appears in.

The mind can't grasp or understand no-thing. The mind, being a "thing" in awareness, is dualistic in that it can only think in terms of opposites. It continually divides, condemns, resists and evaluates absolutely everything based on familiar and associative patterns from the past.

How can the thinking mind, which can only think dualistically, apprehend the non-dual that it is cradled in? It cannot; it can only bow to its source in silence.

You are the Non-dual Space of Awareness that embraces all duality. You are the Non-dual Absolute that all duality arises in.

Mind will never realize *This* cannot be approached with thought, but keeps looking anyway. It doesn't occur to the mind that perhaps it isn't found within its domain. YOU know this already.

Thought (thinking) happens within the changeless presence of awareness that you are. Without you, awareness, thinking could not arise. Consequently, thinking has no independent existence apart from the awareness it arises in.

Apart from thinking, what mind is there? Where is it? Might the mind just be a concept, like the "me" thought? Look for yourself and don't assume or believe. What does present evidence reveal?

Seeing is *never* a matter of thinking!

Like belief, imagination and desire, thought is an object in awareness that comes and goes. If it can be seen, it is an object. If it can be known, it must be an object. This is why what you ARE can never be known.

If you could "know" what you are, you'd have to be an object. You are the Subject that contains all objects, including thinking. Being the One without a second, You are the objects that appear as well.

What you are encompasses the mind and therefore, the mind will never see that which contains it – and that which produced it.

It can never be what you *think* it is because this recognition isn't found in time or thought, nor can it be approached by thought. You are prior to thought – and that which contains thought. This is only discovered or realized in the timeless present.

As Saint Francis of Assisi put it, *"What you're looking for is what's looking."* You cannot look for this because it is doing the looking. You cannot see this precisely because it is doing the seeing. You cannot find this precisely because only an object can be found. You cannot find this because it is doing the finding.

If it is witnessed and known, it must be a "thing" – and a thing is an object. If it can't be seen or known, it is no-thing. Therefore, thinking is an object in awareness. See that it is not the mind that is aware of the mind thinking. If you can be aware of thinking, you must be before the mind.

Your True Nature is not an object that can be conceptualized or known by the five senses. Being beyond the senses, you can't experience what you are. You can only be what you are.

I am not living "my" life. I am being lived by the One Life. There's nobody home here but a welcoming presence. This presence appears to be personal, but it's impersonal. What I really am – and not what I appear to be, is a lover of what is, not a lover of what could be.

Nothing needs to happen or change for me to be what I already am. I am the Source of Wholeness itself, temporarily appearing in the form of a human being, non-separate from anything at all. I am here to express and enjoy what I am – the inexpressible, infinite All That Is.

I am not my mind, my body, my feelings or my experiences. I am not my life story, nor am I an image of myself. I am the boundless aliveness that is both empty and full at the same time. I am that which transcends and includes absolutely everything, never divided, only united.

I am the no-thing that is everything, and nothing is more sacred or holier than what I am. All is an equal expression of that which I Am. I don't own anything, nor do I identify with anything – even what I Am.

You can't find me, but there is no place that I am not. I am freedom itself, the silent aware presence that allows existence to be. I am the freedom that everyone is looking for, but can't find.

I don't live in this world, nor do I 'have' a world. The world is within what I am. The seen world is simply a manifestation of what I am, forever coming and going.

What is born must die. I was never born and I will never die. This body and mind will inevitably perish, but it is not what I Am. What is seen perishes, but what sees is imperishable.

There is only Source appearing, the one appearing as two, the no-thing appearing as everything. I am the Timeless, Impersonal Source that appears as the apparent personal in time.

I am That Which Cannot Be Named; I am the unchanging, still Source where constant change happens within. I am the Absolute Emptiness in which the mind and all appearance collapses in, and then projects itself, within itself, back into the world of objective phenomenon.

## chapter 7

# Without A Reference Point

Bringing your attention to this moment, what do you find? What is happening? Do you find a fixed, unchanging, solid entity called "you" present – or do you find that everything is in constant flux, changing from moment to moment? Do you see any solidity, or do you see a never-ending dance of movement in the form of thinking, feeling, sensation and experience?

Can it be seen that the formless dance happens by itself? Can it be seen that all appearance and experience happens in the vast, open space you are? If there is no person present, can you claim ownership of anything at all?

If we simply notice what is going on in our direct experience, we can feel the heart beating and the lungs breathing. We notice the eyes already seeing and the ears already hearing. We can witness the mind alternating back and forth between thinking and silence. We can notice we don't decide when to think or what to think. We can notice decisions and actions happening all by themselves. We see it all happens by itself and is in fact, One Cosmic Dance.

Is there a dancer doing the dance, or is there only the dance? Have you ever *really* looked?

All manifestation is often said to be the play of Consciousness – or *Lila*. Only Consciousness is truly present, and its magnificent nature is to pretend it's not pretending. It is apparent that you are compelled to dance out your part of the Divine play, until you awaken to the discovery that there's never been any difference between you as the Dancer and you as the Dance.

If you are the one in control of your thinking, why don't you just stop thinking for a day? Too long, you say? Okay, let's make it much simpler. You're in control, so stop thinking for five minutes. How far did you get? A few seconds, maybe? That's it? And you claim you are directing your life?

If you choose your thoughts, why would you ever choose negative, self-defeating thoughts? If you choose your thoughts, you'd always choose happy and loving thoughts, wouldn't you? Since I don't choose my thoughts, I don't choose my decisions, either. Therefore, I am not the doer.

Most people, if they *really* look, can admit that thinking happens all by itself – and that they don't choose their thoughts, but will have a very difficult time seeing that they don't make decisions. To admit this would be to admit they have no control. And the mind is all about control.

Since the mind can't fathom this, it concludes that things would fall apart. It reasons that in order to live a 'balanced' life, it needs to be in control of its environment, in a constant negotiation with its environment. Nothing could be further from the truth.

Life continues as it always has, but in the absence of a believed in separate entity pulling the strings. Life happens, to no one.

The reality is Life is so much more capable of handling things than 'you' will ever be. Life is so much wiser than 'you' will ever be. When thinking ceases, does Life fall apart?

Choices are made, but there isn't a chooser. Decisions are made, but there isn't a decider. Thinking happens, but there is no thinker. Seeing happens, but there is no seer. Hearing happens, but there is no hearer. Smelling happens, but there is no smeller.

Life becomes a miracle as soon as it is seen that Consciousness is not personal, but universal. Life becomes more like a symphony with an endless crescendo, dancing as the appearance of separate person going somewhere. While there is still an apparent individual thinking defeating thoughts, happy thoughts, clever thoughts, the melody plays on, uninter- rupted and unconcerned.

Once it is seen that there is no personal entity, personal thoughts have no solid ground to stand on. You see them for what they are, vibrations of energy inseparable from the impersonal Awareness You Are.

Feelings may still arise, but we don't label or turn them into thoughts. Like bubbles in boiling water, they come up, but when the source of the heat is gone, they dissolve back into where they came from. YOU are where they came from.

If we look a bit closer, we see that none of it is of our own conscious doing – and that it never was – and that all of it is simply a spontaneous dance unfolding all on its own.

Just as you didn't get to decide who your parents are, you didn't get to decide on your particular set of wants, needs and desires, either. We don't create what we want to do, need to do, or capable to do. Conversely, we don't decide on what we don't want, don't need and aren't capable of.

You have never 'done' anything in life, yet you pretend you are the one pulling your own strings! You pretend to be the captain of your own ship! The mind fears seeing this, but You don't.

All the while a non-dual happening unfolds dualistically. It's one formless dance, appearing to play the game of two, effortlessly and spontaneously unfolding as the ever-changing aliveness of this moment.

The only thing that doesn't change witnesses all of it coming and going. The one constant throughout is the ever-present witnessing awareness that you are, that which everything emerges from and returns to.

You can't *believe* you are the Source. You can, but it doesn't mean anything, because you don't know it. In other words, there won't be any lasting byproducts (or fruits) from that belief. You can only *realize* you are the Source. Belief is of the mind and realization is of the heart, or Spirit, that you are.

And so, the difficulty with telling someone they ARE the Source is that the mind will hear that and think that they, as a separate individual, *are* the source. However, this has nothing to do with individuality. This has nothing to do with the "me."

This message is for That which is beyond the mind. You know this already. This isn't "me" writing to "you." This is YOU sending a message to your Self, reminding YOU of what YOU already know, but have simply forgotten. There is no "you" sitting there reading what "I" have written.

How many people want to see that they are Mr. or Mrs. Nobody with no real life purpose or meaning other than to awaken to the dream? Naturally, all this speculation happens before realization. Upon realization, all that was invested in won't be cared about anymore.

Not many want to lose their life in order to save it, especially those who have a relatively happy life, fulfilling most of their wants, needs and desires. Most that live a 'pretty good life' are content with the status quo. A comfortable dream is much more acceptable than a nightmare.

Saint Paul used to say, *"I die daily."* Saint Francis of Assisi said, *"It is only by dying that I can have eternal life."* These men weren't talking about physical death. They were talking about the fictitious self-center most believe themselves to be. They were talking about dying to the beliefs and concepts most take to be real.

The body isn't separate from the elements; it is made of the elements. How would the body hold up without water?  How would the body fare without space and body heat? Could it walk and talk and function if it wasn't in the appearance of matter? You'd be a ghost if it weren't for the appearance of matter!

The body would be dead without being in unison with all of these elements.  The body cannot be separate from the elements, just as the mind can't be separate from the illusory world it believes in.

The same source intelligence-energy that drives the entire universe, the earth to rotate on its axis, that placed the sun at the right distance from the earth to support life, is the very same intelligence that is beating your heart right now, breathing through your lungs right now, growing your hair and fingernails – and seeing through your eyes right now.

If you are absolutely honest when looking – and earnestly desire to see what's really so, you'll find that all there is, is just space. There is no one there when you look. There's just an aware Space in which everything happens, in which everything arises in and falls back into.

No one who has ever really looked (in a non-conceptual way) has ever located the "me" they always assumed was present. All they can do is come up with a bunch of concepts and beliefs about who they think they are. And I'm going to go out on a limb here and guess you didn't find "you," either.

In your actual experience before thought, can you negate this non-finding?

Isn't the only appropriate and *honest* thing you can say, without referring to belief or thought is, "There's just an empty and vast aware Space in which all things are apparently happening in?"

Can you *still* get a sense of moving behind the *appearance* of that guy or gal who's been around for a while, the guy or gal with attributes and qualities, an age, sexual orientation and race, with all the successes and failures – and all the happy and sad times?

And just behind that *appearance* of that guy or gal who's been around for a while is the one who *knows* that guy or gal. You know this; you *know* that there's something just behind, don't you? You *know* there's something just behind "you," silently watching "you" sitting there and reading this – don't you?

Look without conceptualizing.

Disregard belief, assumption and opinion for a moment and look in your actual experience and tell me what you see? Remember not to use any words, assumptions or beliefs.

Can you find a solid entity called "you" – or do you find just a silent, aware presence, without any form and name?  If you can't find "you," do you think that it's a gigantic, unwarranted leap to recognize that You are the Timeless, Nameless, Formless Being that allows all names and forms to appear and disappear in?

If "you" think "you" are contained within the lining of "your" skin, how is it possible to get a sense that there is something just behind "you," silently watching "you" – perhaps in confusion right now, or in peaceful delight right now?

Don't you get a sense of this? Don't you get a *real knowing sense* – and not just a *believed in, 'well maybe'* sense?

It may be disorienting and confusing at first, but so what? Is the awareness OF confusion confused? Is the awareness OF disorientation disoriented? What exactly are feelings anyway? Feelings are simply vibrating energy – energy in motion – coming and going within the ever-present, unchanging being that you are.

On present evidence, is there a 'you' that sees the moon – or is there simply the seeing of the moon? Now drop the concept of 'the moon' and what's left? What's left when the one who sees collapses into what is seen?

This is about looking deeply into your own experience – and then telling the truth. If you don't know, admit you don't know – until you can know. Because I must tell you, you *do* know.

No-boundary awareness is direct, immediate and non-conceptual. It is absolutely uncompromising and not mere philosophical theory. This is why the Sages and Mystics all agree that Reality is beyond name and form, beyond words and descriptions – and beyond division and boundary.

When it is finally seen, beyond belief, what you are, it's not that you are suddenly in possession of extraordinary powers and psychic abilities. You don't necessarily become the most compassionate person in the world, either – nor do you walk around in constant bliss, showering everyone you meet with love beyond measure.

Life goes on as before, only now it is without the inner division and struggle. Resistance can still come up, but it is seen through rather quickly. You don't wish it were any different. As a result, suffering doesn't arise.

Illusion doesn't mean it isn't there. Illusion means that it appears and disappears with a particular life span and therefore, can't be real. While you appear to be a separate person with a separate soul, you are in fact, the One Soul appearing as a separate person.

There's only one thing going on. There is only One Being in many forms, none of which are separate from each other. This is the 'enlightenment' you are looking to discover. In truth there is One Singular Consciousness peering through the eyes of ALL life, including the most tyrannical dictator to the most compassionate person.

Silence is the singular source out of which everything springs from, abides in, and returns to. It is the formless, underlying essence that continually gives birth to thought forms, like the ocean continually gives birth to waves. As no wave ever harms the ocean, no thought or action can ever impact what you really are.

Always arising and falling, waves arise from the source ocean, always being an expression of the ocean. Upon returning to the ocean, they forever remain one with the ocean.

Though it appears the wave "returns" to the ocean, it never left the ocean. Wave and ocean are inseparably one. Silence, thought and activity are one. Silence is not the opposition to thought, noise and activity, but the ever-present, unchanging background of all thought, noise and activity.

Nothing ever obstructs this silence. Nothing *can* obstruct the silence you are. You see that no thought can disrupt the Silent, Awake Being that is your Original Nature. Why would the ocean mind if it has big waves or little waves, whether its surface is calm or turbulent?

Silence is prior to, in the midst of, and after each thought, feeling and activity. It never leaves. It is here right now as you read this. Ever-changing weather simply passes through the background of the empty, silent sky. Changing thoughts, feelings and activity appears in the unchanging, background of the ever-present silence you are.

Notice that the mind reverts back to silence spontaneously after each experience. Simply notice that every experience happens within an ever-present background of silence. Without silence, nothing is. Listen to the silence you are, and trace all thinking, feeling and activity back to its source.

If you relax your gaze and take in the entire visual field, without moving your eyes, allow yourself to become aware of the edges of the visual field. You'll notice an oval-shaped window that you're looking out of. You are indeed looking through a single eye, not the two you've assumed for so long.

Your whole life you've *believed* that you've been looking through two eyes, but in reality, you haven't. If you really *see*, you'll see that all along you've been looking through one eye and not the two you believed in. Granted, you possess two separate eyeballs and can see through both, but in essence and not appearance, you are looking through a single, oval-shaped eye. Relax your gaze and see this.

chapter 8
# A Homecoming

Life and death are two sides of the same coin. Without death, there is no life. What could be more natural than the physical death of something that is born to die? What could be more natural than the death of that which was never meant for eternal life? How can that which is made of perishable stuff survive?

Are we really locked inside the prison of our body/mind, or are we the unbounded awareness that the body is within? Are we really a separate personality with a separate mind trying to make our lives work? See that what you are is not inside of the perishable body – but that the perishable body is inside you.

When we can see our body and notice thinking occurring, being the witness of them, are we not already inextricably free from all movement and sensation? Are we not *already* free and clear from what we witness?

When we rest in the witnessing awareness, watching all thoughts and sensations passing through, can we not sense the innate freedom and release, a sense of not being bound by the continuous parade of concepts and images witnessed?

Resting in the clear and open space of awareness, can we see that the Original Witnessing is not "out there" in the stream of time and objects? Can we see that what we are is the vast and empty background in which all the streams of time and objects arise?

Consciousness was not created with the body – and will not perish after the body dies. In fact, it never enters the stream of time and therefore, isn't subject to death. It does not live on *after* the body dies, for it lives *prior* to the body. Because it is Unborn, it is Undying.

I am the Unborn, Formless Eternal One – the One without a second, in which the cycle of birth and death continually repeats itself. I remain forever untouched and prior to such cycles. I am the One Fountain in which all cycles spring from and repeat.

Suffering is the result of the grasping and avoiding of the separate self, and what ends it is the realization and transcendence of the separate self. Suffering is an inevitable byproduct in the knot or contraction known as the personal self, and the only way to rid suffering is to see through the illusion of the personal self. Seen through, painful experiences no longer own you anymore; they aren't a problem.

The death of the body/mind is essentially the ending of the dream of separation and individuality; it is the ending of the story of a "me" that was trying to always make its life work, journeying a path in time, focused on becoming the 'best person' it could become.

What dies is the firm conviction that you are a separate entity living in a world apart from you, that you are a body/mind organism with name and form. What follows physical death is the resurrection and realization of what you've always been.

Upon physical death, all ideas of heaven, hell, the afterlife, reincarnation, karma, reward and sin end in the clear recognition that there was never anyone living a life and therefore, these concepts never applied. All ideas of here and there, now and then, and before and after, die in the realization there's only a timeless now, without any location.

No longer feeling that you are an entity located inside a body here and now, it is seen that there is only a timeless presence, not a 'now' – and 'here' as location-less presence, and not any location in space. No experiencer and no experience. There's only This – and it is beyond time. The emptiness of Consciousness recognizes itself as the fullness of This.

Wholly unconcerned, yet intimately engaged, there is absolutely nothing to fear or recoil from, for you are each and every thing, entirely and completely. Everything you look at is what you are, and in this boundless seeing, you are released from everything you were once bound by.

You are the love and beauty you've been seeking. Being Home is the realization that the substance of your Home is *built* from Love and Beauty. Love is the discovery that others are not others. Beauty is the discovery that objects are not objects. Love and beauty is what you are.

When it is seen that you are before the mind – and when it is seen that the mind is an object in Consciousness that is known, the mind has a tendency to quiet down. In silence, the mind finally sees its limitations and bows to its source, knowing its true place and function.

Resting in the simple, clear and alive presence of awareness that everything is dependent upon, there is an extraordinary absence of the person you used to think you were. In that absence is a presence intimate with all that arises. You are the open, unchanging capacity for all things to intimately arise in.

What you are has no need to alter this moment. It has no need to be certain of anything, for you are the certainty in the uncertainty – and you are the uncertainty in the certainty. What you are bathes in the wonder of the unknown. All uncertainty is fully embraced in the Certainty you are. If this moment is unknown, with an infinite potential of outcomes, how can the moment be predetermined?

Although whatever arises cannot be any other way than it is, this inevitable moment doesn't imply destiny. If there is any destiny, it is in the "things are always as they are" Reality. This is what Anthony de Mello meant when he described enlightenment as an *"absolute cooperation with the inevitable."*

All thoughts, feelings and sensations appearing presently are already welcome in the vast, open, container that you are. Nothing is preferred or denied entry; nothing needs to be modified or improved.

Nothing needs to be purified, forgiven or worked through. This moment is whole and complete, as it is.

There is no place like Home. Even if you feel you aren't Home, you never left Home. There has never been any real obstacle in the way of you being Home. It is only a thought that divides the seamless totality of experience into an experiencer and the experienced.

You are the untouched, timeless Home for all time-bound experience to rest in, no matter how painful or frightening. Whatever arises is being fully embraced – by what you are. You don't need to "do" surrender. Simply and effortlessly notice surrender is what you already are.

The mind's resistance or rejection to anything that arises is an afterthought, a delayed response to what already is, to what is already being allowed. The mind's reactions and interpretations are totally irrelevant to what you really are – and can never contaminate the empty Space of Awareness You Are.

When it is seen that you aren't who you believed yourself to be, you're no longer a person with a background or history. You're not a man, woman, father, mother, brother, sister, son or daughter. You are not a husband, wife, Christian, Jew, Buddhist, Hindu, Muslim, agnostic or atheist.

You're not Black, White, Asian, Indian, Latino or any other race. You're not a happy or depressed person. You aren't a rich or poor person, a successful or unsuccessful person. You are not your body or mind that will one day perish.

You are Life itself; never were you an individual entity possessing a life. You never lived in this world; the world was always within you. You are the awareness that is inseparable from everything that arises in awareness. Not only are you the awareness of all that arises, you are what arises, too. Everything that appears is made of the Same Singular Substance.

Like the wave that reaches the shoreline ceasing to be a wave, it is revealed to be the Ocean all along. Seeking and thoughts of resistance and desire cease in the clear light of understanding, and is revealed to be sourced in that which produced it – the clear, open space of presence you are. That Space is the Home that cannot be named or described.

Even if identification happens with an illusory individual, you are no less the One Life, appearing as a seemingly separate individual.  While it appears personal, there is nothing personal unfolding.  You aren't doing any of it, including reading or trying to understand this right now.

From the old man shuffling down the street pushing a cart of groceries, the wrinkles in your father's skin, your heart breaking at the thought of your dear mother trying to come to terms with a progressive, incurable disease, a homeless man in tattered clothes rummaging through a dumpster for food, to a mother breast feeding her baby – all that you see is what you are.

If you deny this, it simply means you just believed a thought in your mind.  It simply means that you believe the thoughts in your head *as* Reality, and that you believe separation *is* the Reality. How can you deny what you don't understand and yet see? What sense does it make to reference the temporal, death-bound and dependent mind for Truth or Reality?

It is anger arising at the sight of an elderly woman being pushed out of the way by a middle-aged man trying to pass her down the steps, and finding yourself rushing over to make sure she doesn't fall, because you had no choice, and you never did have any choice.

Seeing that you were never once separate from anything, that you never once chose your thoughts and behaviors, you finally see that choice and free will are illusory. Finally seeing that you are being lived by the One Life, and that you never had a life, the contracted energy of the fictitious self disperses back into the boundless energy you've always been.

In that dispersing, a radical shift in perception occurs and you're no longer identified with the 'I' thought and the body. You *see* what Jesus meant when he made the statement, *"I and my Father are One"* – and Saint Francis of Assisi's pointer, *"What you're looking for is what is looking."* Like Buddha, it makes you tilt your head to the sky and laugh out loud.

What I was looking for was here all along, closer than breathing, nearer than hands and feet – and it was doing the looking! "Who" would of thought?! What a great place to hide something so obvious. No wonder it was overlooked for so long! *"He is hidden in His manifestation, manifest in His concealing."*

All the pent up guilt, shame, blame, resentment and remorse accumulated from an imagined past simply dissolves in the clear recognition that none of it is real, and none of it was ever real, including the "you" that imagined all that – including a "you" with a past, present or future. You are the timeless now that everything arises in. Not only are you this moment, you are all that arises *in* this moment.

In place of insecurity and low self-esteem, absolute security and a complete absence of *any* self-esteem whatsoever moves in. Where before you had a lingering sense of incompleteness and inadequacy, now there is an abiding sense of fullness – and a deep OK-ness with what is, as it is.

No teachers, no students. No awake or unawake beings. No path or absence of a path. Simply life loving itself, spontaneously dancing all by itself, appearing as the seen and unseen, rising and falling back into the empty, aware, knowing Space that allows it all to be, eternally.

There's no place like Home. Only a separate mind would desire more. Only a separate mind would desire something other. You're already Home. You know you're Home when the question whether or not you're Home drops away. Since you're Home, there's nowhere to go.

Can you do me a small favor and leave an honest review?  The more reviews, the more Amazon promotes the book and thus, more people see the book!

Simply go back to the page where you purchased it and click on the link that reads, "Write a review."

Thank you.

www.ingramcontent.com/pod-product-compliance
Lightning Source LLC
Chambersburg PA
CBHW060017050426
42448CB00012B/2787